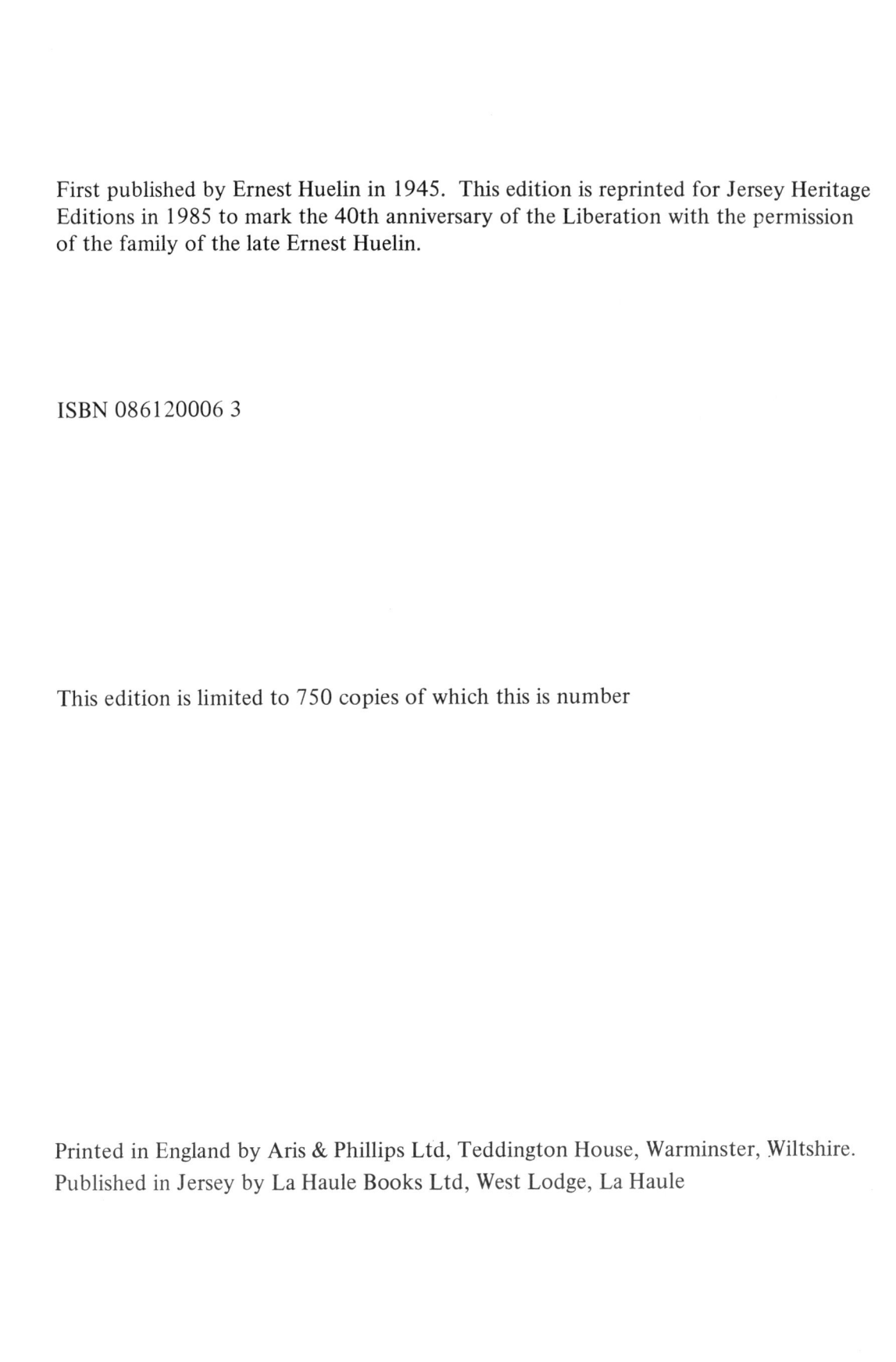

First published by Ernest Huelin in 1945. This edition is reprinted for Jersey Heritage Editions in 1985 to mark the 40th anniversary of the Liberation with the permission of the family of the late Ernest Huelin.

ISBN 086120006 3

This edition is limited to 750 copies of which this is number

Printed in England by Aris & Phillips Ltd, Teddington House, Warminster, Wiltshire.
Published in Jersey by La Haule Books Ltd, West Lodge, La Haule

JERSEY IN JAIL
1940~45

BY HORACE WYATT
PICTURES BY
EDMUND BLAMPIED

The Author and Artist who have worked together in the production of this book have asked me to write its dedication. Having acted in the guise of prisoners' friend, and adviser to my two friends Horace Wyatt and Edmund Blampied, this gives me extreme pleasure.

I therefore, without hesitation, dedicate "Jersey in Jail" to the "Housewives of Jersey" who, in spite of ever-increasing difficulties and with ever-decreasing supplies, both of food and fuel, kept the home fires burning and saw their families through a most trying ordeal.

ERNEST HUELIN.

Jersey, 1945.

INTRODUCTION

THIS book does not profess to be a history of the German Occupation of the Channel Islands, or an important contribution to the literature of the War. In the series of "Unposted Letters" which are scattered through it, I have tried merely to give, in brief, some idea of what life was like in the only part of the British Empire invaded and held by Germany and to outline our predominant feelings at various stages. In so doing I have avoided expressing any opinions on controversial matters connected with local politics.

In my effort to escape giving a thoroughly boring description of what was generally a thoroughly boring existence, I have aimed at brevity and variety of treatment, sprinkling rhymes about among the prose. These rhymes have one characteristic in common with Blampied's admirable illustrations and, I fear, only one. This is that some of them are intended to be taken seriously, while others are purely frivolous or satirical. As regards quality in either sphere, I cannot hope to have done more than provide a fairly innocuous background, against which the brilliance of Blampied's beautiful or humorous work can show up to advantage.

If my rough sketches, in prose and verse, while supplying this background, serve also to refresh the fading memories of those who were in Jersey during the Occupation and to give others some slight impression of the outstanding angles of an unpleasant and fortunately unique experience, they will achieve all I dare to hope for them.

For the rest, "Jersey in Jail" can, at least, claim to be a Hundred-per-cent. Jersey product. It was written and illustrated in Jersey, during the Occupation.

HORACE WYATT.

Jersey, 1945.

[NOTE.—The verses on pages 7, 18, 68, 70, 84, 91 and 92 were written for the Symphonic Cantata, 'Liberi Gaudeamus,' composed by Mr. P. G. Larbalestier, for Post-War production in Jersey and elsewhere.

The verses on pages 78, 80 and 81 were written for inclusion, as a recitation, in the programme of a Concert organised, early in 1945, in Jersey, in aid of the funds of the Red Cross Society.]

Our Island, prone beneath a hostile heel,
Is but a prison. The surrounding sea
No longer beckons to the traveller,
No longer links the wanderer with his home;
But shapes itself a moat impassable,
A deep-filled ditch around the dungeon walls,
Holding the captive as securely caged
As bolts and bars of iron.
                        The clock ticks on:
The long, lean years go slowly limping by,
In purposeless depression.
                        Only those
Who have been prisoned know what Freedom means!

UNPOSTED LETTER No. 1.   July, 1940.

THE GERMANS OCCUPY JERSEY

Jersey is in Jail! The little Islands that were William the Conqueror's before ever he fought at Hastings, the oldest inheritance of England's king, are, for the time being, under the heel of England's arch-enemy.

On June 19th, 1940, we were told that the States of Jersey (our local Governing Body) had been officially notified by the British Government that it had been decided to declare the Channel Islands a "demilitarised zone." Now that the Germans' rapid westerly drive along the North of France had brought them to the coast of the Cotentin, it was obvious that Jersey had lost any little strategic value that might have been ours till then. With the enemy holding the mainland within sight of us, only a few miles away, we, with our one little airfield, were wide open to overwhelming aerial attacks, against which we could put up no sort of adequate defence.

Now we understood well enough that the idea of any defence at all must be given up and the British troops and planes withdrawn. As to what else might be implied by such phrases as "demilitarised zone" or "open town," few if any of us had any very distinct notion. All we had to go by was a statement that facilities were being provided for the "voluntary evacuation" of a certain number of civilians. These facilities, we were told, were to be offered first to women and children; next, if still possible, to men of military value; and finally to any others for whom shipping space could be provided. The form in which these plans were made known was, perhaps, a little unfortunate. It savoured strongly of the time-honoured principle, "save the women and children," and so rather tended to create the impression that things looked very black for those who might be left behind, and this was inclined to produce panic and to reflect unfairly on some of the men who decided to leave.

During the following morning the Bailiff of Jersey (our Chief Executive) and other officials tried to steady the nerves of the populace, publicly advising the majority to stay in the Island. This, naturally, could not apply to those in the active services and the reserves, and the Lieutenant-Governor and the Militia left on the 21st. Meanwhile, hundreds of farms and private houses had been hastily evacuated and a great many domestic animals and cars left ownerless. In many other cases, men sent their wives and families to England and remained in Jersey themselves. Altogether, some eight to ten thousand, out of a total of about fifty thousand, left the island.

By the 22nd the people as a whole were recovering from the shock and life was so nearly returning to the normal that the export of potatoes to England had begun again, while, a day or so later, it was announced that mailboats would henceforth run "only twice a week."

This, in itself, is sufficient to show how far nearly everyone was from understanding the position. But the natural assumption that the continuance of the export trade and of the mail service meant that no complete severance from Great Britain was to be immediately expected, was soon shown to be wrong.

On the 27th, German planes flew over at a low level and had a good look at what was going on in the Harbour, where the shipping of potatoes was in full swing. The fact that no guns went into action against them should have told the pilots again what they must have known already: that the Island was undefended.

However this may be, they paid us a further visit the following afternoon. This time they bombed the fishing village of La Rocque on the South-East coast, machine-gunned the roads as they passed Westward, and finally dropped a number of bombs in and around the harbour of St. Helier, causing a considerable number of casualties, many of them fatal, and doing a great deal of material damage,† chiefly to Hotels and quay-side Warehouses.

This exploit was described in the German official wireless news as an attack on "troop embarkations and concentrations of army transport"; this despite the facts that none of the lorries about the harbour carried anything more deadly than the common potato, all troops had left the Island about a week before and St. Helier had been proclaimed an "open town" not later than June 19th. No doubt the real object of the raid was to "put the wind up" the population and so discourage any hostile demonstration when the Germans should see fit to land.

This they actually did, from planes, on July 1st, under circumstances as prosaic and devoid of glamour as was conceivably possible. Nevertheless, some most absurd fairy-stories were promptly concocted for the delectation of the German people. According to one of these, printed in a paper of theirs, a young German airman displayed astonishing courage, actually capturing the Island single-handed at prodigious personal risk!

What really happened was, briefly, as follows. At no greater risk than is run by anyone who travels a few miles by air in peace-time, planes dropped

† Afterwards found to amount to near £100,000.

messages to the local authorities, giving directions as to various steps which must be taken to show that no resistance would be offered, and stipulating that certain officials were to meet the invaders at the air-field. With these directions came a proclamation, over the signature of General Von Richthoven, Commander of the German Air Forces in Normandy, which was promptly posted up all over the Island, with the Bailiff's instructions that no resistance was to be offered.

In this proclamation the German Commander announced his intention of "neutralising military establishments" and gave a warning of the consequences that would follow any hostile action. He then finished up with the categorical statement—

"In case of peaceful surrender the lives, property and liberty of peaceful inhabitants are solemnly guaranteed."

We shall find out later on how much this promise really means! Meanwhile, all instructions were carried out to the letter and later in the day German officers and men arrived and were duly met and escorted from the air-field to the town, where they established temporary headquarters at the Town Hall.

The populace, throughout, did exactly as was required of them. There were no disturbances or demonstrations of any kind and, generally speaking, people seemed more stunned than excited. In fact, the prescribed "peaceful surrender," being quite unavoidable, was silent and automatic.

The Swastika is flying from Fort Regent and Elizabeth Castle. German troops are marching through our streets, rejoicing by numbers, singing at the word of command. The Nazi occupation of Jersey has begun.

THE GERMANS OCCUPY JERSEY.

A GERMAN OFFICER TO HIS TROOPS, 1940.

Sing, all you mis-begotten bounders, Sing,
Let raucous melody resound afar!
Sing like the deuce—and make the welkin ring
(Whatever " welkins " are).
Go gaily warbling down the dismal street
And see that every Jerry that you meet
Raises his hand to give the appointed sign
That Adolf is divine,
And breathes in awe-struck syllables the while
The mighty words of doom—" Heil! Hitler! Heil! "—
Sing, Damn you! Let your cry be loud and stirring!
    Go goebelling on! In ecstasy go goering!
        Your loyal himmlers sing,
            Like anything!

[When the following lines were added in 1944, the quality of the troops had considerably deteriorated and they had a good deal less to sing about.]

Come! Sing; confound you! Make it bright and snappy!
At least let other people think you're happy!
Sing, damn you! All you bleak, lugubrious blighters
Do try and look like fighters;
You wretched, gawky, rotten, C.3 crowd;
Sing loud!
Adjust your goggles! Straighten up your backs,
Beneath their laden packs!
Move your flat feet as if you really saw
A happy termination to your war!
    Hittle like hell! Go hoarsely carolling!
      And sing, you miserable bastards! SING!

SING, ALL YOU MIS-BEGOTTEN BOUNDERS, SING.

Unposted Letter No. 2.   *Jan., 1941.*

EARLY RE-ACTIONS

Well, we have now been " occupied " for six months ! When the Germans first arrived here, they boasted freely that they would be all over England in six *weeks*. Some of the more ignorant thought Jersey was the Isle of Wight and that they would presently reach the mainland by wading ! An officer quartered at one of our hotels chaffingly asked his waiter at what hours his meals would be served in London, to which the man replied with polite regret that he was unacquainted with British prison regulations.

Now that they have fought and lost the aerial battle of London their tone is rather less confident. Some, I am told, even go so far as to admit that we " may get them in the end." But that end must surely be far off as yet, in spite of the rather parochial view held by some people and typified by an old lady whom I heard saying, " But, my dear ! It *can't* last more than another three months. Why ! *Jersey* could never stand it ! "

Meanwhile, we begin to experience the horror of ignorance. We know that the German attack on London has, broadly speaking, failed ; that the Cockneys have said, and shown, that they can " take it." We do *not* know how long is the casualty list ; what famous names, what names of our own relations and friends, figure in it. We are oppressed by doubts and fears. We know, too, that many fine relics of the past must have been wiped out. We do *not* know if our mental picture of the devastation is an exaggeration or an under-estimate. But it is the loss of the people rather than of the buildings, that weighs most heavily upon us.

JERSEY COULD NEVER STAND IT!

Grieve not, if in the lands we prize,
The cities we adore,
Old landmarks fail to greet returning eyes,
Known beauties shine no more.
New towers to greater heights shall grow,
Swift spires shall seek the stars,
Above the old, the battered, walls that show
Their honourable scars.

And all the crowded homes of men
That war's rude hands have torn,
Shall rise in shapelier resurrection then:
New-built for men new-born;
While, in the aftermath of ire,
In right distilled from wrong,
Our sons, like steel fierce-fashioned in the fire,
Shall stand more straight, more strong.

In general, the "Army of Occupation" consists of well set up men, apparently in first-class condition and certainly showing no signs of a starved infancy following the last war, or of the ill-effects of more recent years of "ersatz" feeding. Their superficial manners are, on the whole, good. We have seen German officers treat their men in a contemptuous and sometimes brutal way that would be inconceivable in the British Army, but the behaviour of all ranks towards civilians here has, up to now, been almost always polite and ingratiating. The absence of the "Prussian Jack-boot" manner has been an agreeable surprise. Evidently orders have been given to establish friendly relations with the people of occupied territories and, if possible, persuade them that German occupation is something of a blessing and the Nazi regime gentle and considerate.

Also, on the whole, the restrictions imposed have not yet been excessive, being more or less confined to the imposition of a curfew, a stringent black-out and strict limitation of facilities for fishing. Regulations on this last subject have been frequent, changeable and cumulative, with the result that the supply of fish, except to the Germans themselves, soon became quite negligible.*

The attitude of the Jersey people towards the invaders has, generally speaking, been polite but firmly aloof. Some of the young officers tried hard at first to establish social relations by organising dances, concerts, and so on, to which civilians were invited. After a time, however, their efforts died away for want of adequate response, other than from the least desirable and reputable sections of the community. In this last class, a certain number of girls, and of young married women who should have known better, have—as I suppose always happens—welcomed the overtures of anything in uniform and I am afraid that there will be serious trouble in certain households when the men return from war service, particularly as Jersey Law does not recognise divorce.

During the first week or so of the occupation there was a rush on the shops and, naturally enough in a place almost entirely dependent on imports, stocks of most things in everyday use were soon exhausted. This tendency became evident very quickly; so much so that, as early as August, a Delegation went to France to buy "essential commodities," and consignments of food-stuffs in fact began to arrive in September, though they were by no means ideal as regards either quantity or variety. In October all shops dealing in clothing, footwear and soap were closed for ten days and when they re-opened textiles and leather goods were strictly rationed and almost impossible to get and soap had disappeared from the market altogether.†

---

* Throughout the Occupation fish was almost always unobtainable.

† Later on, a gritty material from France, quite destitute of fat and giving no lather, was occasionally distributed as a ration up to the time of the 1944 invasion of Europe. After that, there was no soap at all, either for personal or for household use.

The town is, of course, very dull. The shops, which in any case are nearly empty, are only allowed to open from 10 to 12.30 and from 2 to 4.30, and many are closed altogether or for two or three days in the week. Many shop windows are boarded up. As to the shops' contents, most things that we used to take for granted are already nearly, or quite, unobtainable. To mention only a few things, taken haphazard, imagine a life steadily becoming devoid of such things as needles, pins, tape, elastic, wool and cotton ; kitchen utensils of every kind ; all facilities for cleaning anything ; tinned foods ; beer and spirits ; tapioca, rice, sago, pearl barley and the like ; pepper, salt, mustard and all other condiments and sauces ; coffee, cocoa, chocolate and sweets of all kinds.

The weekly butter ration is down to two ounces and tea to one ounce. There are no cooking fats to be had. The meat ration, including offal, is 12-oz. a week ; bacon is unobtainable ; eggs pure gold ; while chickens and rabbits still exist in small numbers for millionaires only. There is no jam or marmalade. Baking powder is almost finished. As yet there is no rationing of bread, but the quality is very poor and white flour is a thing of the past. There are, naturally, no fancy cakes, as sugar is one of our rarest luxuries.

There is, of course, an acute shortage of petrol. Private cars are off the road, except those of doctors and a few officials, and bus services have been reduced to a skeleton. As we are wholly dependent on the road for our internal transport, this affects our lives very considerably. Bicycles are fetching fancy prices and, in effect, it is as though our friends were all moving away into the distance.

One of the worst aspects of our position is that nobody comes or goes ; one never meets anyone " new " ; there is nothing fresh—outside the wireless news—to discuss with anyone you *do* meet ; there is no such thing as a new book, a new play, a new film or a new story.

We get frequent occular and oral evidence that "there is a war on," but comparatively little contact with all that is happening. We have no newspaper comment—other than that which is wholly German inspired—to help us clothe the bare bones of news in flesh.

The Germans seem to have been making quite extensive use of our airport which, one hears, is being, or has already been, much enlarged—its vicinity is, of course, forbidden ground. From the first, we saw and heard German planes in small numbers passing over day and night and generally flying very low. Then the numbers increased from units to dozens, and the noise in proportion. Sometimes they have circled overhead for hours at night time, seemingly using Jersey as a gathering point for squadrons massing for raids on England. Sometimes we have heard gunfire and sometimes the noise of a few bombs. We wonder if, one day, the Island may be the site of a big aerial battle. At times we have thought—whether we have thought rightly I cannot say—that a fair number of our own planes have been over. Certainly, judging from the sound of German guns in action, there have been at least a few, and though one does not fancy the idea of being bombed by our own friends, people have, on the whole, welcomed any such evidences of British activity.

Up to the present, we have had no individual news from Great Britain, but a scheme has been put in motion under which there seems to be a likelihood of getting short personal messages through the Red Cross. Meanwhile, this complete severance from friends, and it may be families, outside the Island is one of the most distressing aspects of our strange position. There is no probability of letters like this one getting through until we have seen the last of our unwelcome visitors. Is it worth while writing them at all? Well, perhaps they may be of some sort of interest to somebody or other, who may be searching for contemporary personal impressions in days to come.

CARTE D'IDENTITÉ.

Where'er I walk, I carry with me now
My " Carte d'Identité," on which are stated
Various details as to where and how
And why and wherefore I was born and mated;
Particulars of hair and eyes (Hair—None;
Eyes—Two); my age upon my date of birth
(No years, point nought);
                        A photograph of one
Of the most horrid criminals on earth
Glares from the centre of the dirty page.
My signature, my birthmarks and my age
Complete the record:
                     So that, any time,
Should I commit some really beastly crime;
Supposing, for example, I should walk
With three or more companions in talk;
Should I remain outdoors five minutes late;
Should I write " V " on someone's garden gate;
Should I set foot upon forbidden ground;
Should I be so unlucky that I'm found
Spending the night—or worse! the whole week-end—
Away from home with some quite harmless friend;
Should it be known that I'm inclined to sing
(Say) " Rule Britannia " or " God Save the King ";
Should I be proved an Oddfellow or Mason
(And sent to " jug " because I am a base 'un)
This " Carte d'Identité," produced in time,
Will serve to fit the culprit to the crime.

Unposted Letter No. 3.   Jan. 1942.

BOREDOM UNUTTERABLE

We are now in the depths of the second winter of our discontent. The weather is unusually severe for Jersey, with alternations of rain and heavy snow, and the discomforts of our position are steadily piling up. All gas fires in sitting rooms, bedrooms and passages have been disconnected. Also all gas-fed water heating and circulating apparatus. Thus gas can only be used for cooking and the hours at which any supply, even for this purpose, is available are strictly limited ; one result being that those who have depended on gas for lighting are left in darkness early in the evening. Candles are at a premium and only a few people have any left.

The solid fuel monthly winter ration of the average house is two hundredweights of wood and one of coal or coke, which means restricting fires to one room and then only lighting up when the cold is very intense. Hot baths are an almost unheard of luxury and hot-water bottles cannot be bought. People are, of course, feeling the cold much more acutely than usual, while subsisting on a diet almost innocent of meat, sugars and fats. Very few have any superfluous fat of their own left on them and, for lack of heating, our houses are getting very damp. Nearly all of us have lost a lot of weight—personally I have gone down about four stone. But, up to now, many—I might almost say, most—of us do not feel any the worse for it. There are certainly some who have positively benefited by the compulsory slimming process, the impossibility of over-eating or taking too much to drink. It has done us good.

The meat ration—inclusive of bones, skin, gristle and offal—has been reduced to eight, and then to four, ounces a week. The male tobacco ration—and tobacco is definitely useful for staying hunger—fluctuates round about 20 cigarettes, or the equivalent in pipe tobacco, a week : women get none at all. Other rations also vary from time to time, but the standard is round about 5 lbs. of bread, 2 ozs. of butter, 2 ozs. of sugar, and—until recently—one oz. of tea a week. Now the tea ration has stopped altogether and the price of tea on the " black market " is soaring. Some people are brewing substitutes out of grated parsnips or beet, or from blackberry leaves. Potatoes are not yet rationed, but there are signs that they will be before long. Over and above our regular rations we get a sort of " surprise packet " nearly every week, as the result of the efforts of our representatives in France. The " extra " varies in kind and quality. A few examples from recent months are :—A cake of (so-called) soap, 4 ozs. of Macaroni, 2 ozs. of cooking fat, 1 lb. of jam, 100 saccharines, 3 ozs. of barley semolina, 4 ozs. of coffee substitute, and a very small tin of Tunny Fish. We hardly ever get two " extras " in one week and sometimes we get none at all. Irregularly, and not as a ration, some Camembert cheeses arrive, but often after such long delays that they are uneatable.

It is almost impossible to buy anything in the way of clothes, except an occasional vest or a pair of socks, and the Island is beginning to manufacture clog-soled boots and shoes.

Petty restrictions and annoyances are steadily piling up, which, I suppose, recognising the German love of organisation in detail, is only to be expected. For instance, we are all " Registered " and nobody is allowed to sleep away from home without giving notice. We have to carry our " Identity Cards " with us everywhere and a list of the inhabitants of every house must be posted inside the front door. The possibility of aerial bombardment seems to be admitted by an order that all attics are to be cleared of inflammable materials. The rule of the road has been altered from the British to the Continental one.

The quality of the occupying troops is not what it was, and they seem to be wavering in their conviction that they have as good as won. But, for all

VERY FEW HAVE ANY SUPERFLUOUS FAT OF THEIR OWN.

that, their confidence not long ago was such that they fully expected to finish with Russia inside two months from the declaration of war. It may be due to the fact that this expectation has been disappointed, like their earlier anticipation of the breakdown of Great Britain, that they seem to be getting more touchy and sensitive.

It is curious to note that the Germans, despite their declared hatred for—one would suppose—all things Semitic, apply the doctrines of the Old rather than the New Testament to their dealings with what they are pleased to regard as "crime." They visit the sins of the individual not upon him alone, but preferably upon all his family and even upon his neighbours who could not conceivably have had the slightest influence on his actions. The idea is to put the fear of the Nazi God into everybody and to discourage misdemeanour by stirring up the wrath of the whole population against the culprit, as the instigator of the penalties imposed on everyone.

Recently some girls committed the heinous crime of writing the letter "V" on a wall or pavement. Until they handed themselves over to justice (?) and were sent to prison for a considerable spell, platoons of local householders had to patrol the district throughout the night and the locality was temporarily deprived of its wireless sets. The Germans have, by the way, countered the "V" campaign by the *tu quoque* method and have been busily painting V's all over their buildings and cars, though what the sign can really signify in German I am at a loss to understand.

Petrol supplies are shorter than ever and the bus services are as curtailed as a Manx Cat. One's friends—those of them who are left here—are becoming more and more inaccessible. One feels rather like an animal in a large cage. The mere fact that you can't get out makes you want to, and there is always an underlying fear that one day the Keeper may forget to bring your meagre dinner. But the lack of variety of food is, to my mind, far less distressing than the lack of variety of companionship and the terrible inadequacy of means

SOME GIRLS COMMITTED THE HEINOUS CRIME OF WRITING THE LETTER "V" ON A WALL.

of communication with anyone outside the Island. Everybody has said, to everybody he knows, everything he thinks about everything there is to talk about so often that everybody is rapidly getting sick of everyone else ; tempers grow short and laughter is nearly extinct.

This, to my mind, is one of the worst factors in the situation : this and the feeling that one is circumscribed, hampered, supervised and overheard, sent back to a boarding school at an age when the restrictions of school life have become unbearable. Moreover, at school one could look forward to holidays at some known date ; here one cannot. There are no " letters from home," beyond terse messages about six months old ; no " hampers " of delicacies ; no visitors from outside to introduce new thoughts and topics ; no " organised games " ; next to nobody with whom to discuss the foibles of one's friends !

All days are exactly alike, except that Thursdays and Sundays are rather worse than the others. On Thursdays the shops close at 12.30 instead of 4.0 and the very limited bus services of other days are further reduced. On Sundays there are no shops and no buses at all. Otherwise, all days are the same. You cannot even—as at school—break bounds and chance the consequences.

The one gleam of light in the otherwise complete darkness of ignorance of current events is the wireless and, mercifully, there seems to be no idea of taking this away from us unless some sort of obstreperous behaviour on our part stirs the wrath of our gaolers. We must, I suppose, be thankful for small mercies and continue to hope that no " naughty boy " will bring down punishment equally on the heads of the just and the unjust.

OR WHAT?

[During the early stages of the Occupation those who owned anything for which there was a big demand got round the law regulating prices by offering their goods, not for sale, but in exchange for some other specified article, " Or what ? "]

Will someone tell me what is " What " ?
It's something that I need a lot ;
Something that, if I had it, would
Procure me everything that's good.
When I survey the " Evening Post,"
The column that attracts me most
Is that which tells about the range
Of treasures offered in exchange
For other things I haven't got
   " Or What ? "

Exchange :—A toothbrush ; nearly new,
For half a pint of liquid glue,
   Or What ?
A box of really good cigars
For gallon of Martell, Three Stars,
   Or What ?
A conscientious objector
For a fat Jurat, or a Rector,
   Or What ?
Exchange :—A Berkshire sow, with litter
For half a dozen casks of bitter,
   Or What ?
Exchange :—Commission in Luftwaffer
For chickens' food† or next best offer,
   Of What ?

† As it was against the law to sell wheat at an exhorbitant price, it was always offered in the " Black Market " under the name of " first-grade—or best—chickens' food."

A month's supply of " ration " meat
For anything that's fit to eat,
   Or What ?
Exchange :—Although the flesh is coarse,
" A horse ! My kingdom for a horse ! "
   Or What ?
Exchange :—For free (or other) pardon
Castle and grounds at Berchtesgarten,
   Or What ?
I know a man who must have got
  A lot
    Of " WHAT."
His cellars bulge with logs and coals,
(While mine are merely full of holes) ;
He owns at least three decent suits,
A Macintosh and Rubber boots ;
His collars' edges haven't gone ;
His cuffs have got no whiskers on.
By close inspection, I have learned
His overcoat has not been turned,
(While mine—that has been turned—I've found
Now buttons up the wrong way round.)

He's the luckiest man in St. Helier ;
 There's nothing he cannot obtain ;
And the reason for this I can tell yer
  Is plain.
He has plenty of food, drink and firing,
 Because he has stored such a lot
Of what everyone is requiring
  That's " WHAT."

"EXCHANGE AND MART."
SOW IN FARROW FOR A VIOLIN—OR WHAT?

For he is the man who replies to
 Advertisements every day
(The small and the medium size too)
 Which say,
" *My worldly possessions, in part, or*
 It may be, the whole bally lot,
I am ready and willing to barter
 For ' WHAT ? ' "

I fear I shall never know what it
 Can be that the public so lacks,
But, whatever " WHAT " is, he has got it,
 Yes ! Sacks ! !

So his coal fires are constantly roaring ;
 He wallows in baths, piping hot ;
And cartloads of timber he's storing,
 For " WHAT ? "

On chops, if they're juicy and fat, or
 On ducklings, or lamb and mint sauce,
Or sirloin he feeds as a matter
 Of course.

Cigarettes he secures by the stack ; o—
 —ver twenty-five " hundreds " he's got ;
And he's scooped seven kegs of tobacco,
 For " WHAT " ?

Good whisky he always keeps handy ;
 His cocktails are potent, but pure ;
With his coffee he sips a large brandy
 Liqueur.

In short, of the men of St. Helier,
 The luckiest bloke of the lot
Is the feller who knows how to tell yer
 What's " WHAT " ?

UNPOSTED LETTER No. 4.   *July, 1942.*

THE DARKNESS DEEPENS

The conditions of our imprisonment differ from those of the ordinary convicted criminal. For one thing, he knows the duration of his sentence and is assured that, provided he behaves himself, the terms of its service, once laid down, will not be arbitrarily varied to his detriment. We, on the other hand, are subject to the whims of that enthusiastic band of sadistic amateurs, the Gestapo, who delight in thinking out new and surprising tortures for their victims and are well aware that mental distress can be made even more unbearable than physical pain.

I remember once reading of a political prisoner who was incarcerated in a cell in the clock-tower of some petty autocrat's palace. At first the cell, though small, had, at least, the advantage of being light. Moreover, the big, barred window gave a wide view, from the full height of the tower, down over the surrounding country.

But after a·few days the prisoner realised that the window was slowly moving upwards ; or, to be more exact, the floor and ceiling of the cell, the whole of which really constituted the weight of the great clock—wound only once a year—were moving *down*.

Gradually the window seemed to get higher and higher. A day came when he could no longer see the land outside, but only a patch of sky. But still he had light, till the falling ceiling began gradually to cut it off. Then the window became smaller every day, and at last he was left in utter darkness, with no knowledge as to when, if ever, he would look upon the light again.

Twelve months ago I nearly mentioned this story, which seemed to have something in common with our own position, hedged around by more and more confining restrictions and irritations. On second thoughts, however, it did not seem a fair simile, since there was no apparent prospect of the removal of the wireless; our only means of—so to speak—looking out over the world. The view it gave was only dim and distant, but so long as we could get it, we could feel that we were not altogether cut off from touch with life.

Now our last ray of light has gone. The little window, through which we have caught momentary glimpses of the landmarks of the great world, has been shuttered. We are in darkness. They have taken away our wireless. We are forbidden to know the truth of current events, to be aware of every day happenings. We are fed solely on the propaganda served up to us by the German editor of our only paper, and carefully calculated to breed pessimism, if not despair. . . .

THE RAPE OF THE WIRELESS.

JUNE, 1942.

This dreary life more dreary grows;
  The days more dull, the nights more bleak,
  Since those damned Huns set out to sneak
Our inoffensive radios.

They kindly tell us (damn their eyes)
  That this is " not a punishment."
  They seem to think that they have sent
An unctuous blessing, in disguise!

No punishment! And yet they choose
  The Channel Isles—and us alone—
  To suffer for some sin unknown,
The only place to get no news!

Except what we absorb, at most,
   From the foul stream of poison-lies,
   Of constant source, but varying size,
Fed to us through "The Evening Post."

But there it is! So now, in vain!
   The clanging notes of old Big Ben
   Resound to give us warning when
The news is "on the air" again.

No more we hear the voice that cries,
   "The Fleet is all lit up!" No more
   The Brain's Trust spills the priceless store
Of Mr. Joad's informed replies.

We must not hear the latest jest,
   The latest song, the latest play,
   The latest slang from U.S.A.,
Or anything of interest.

We must not know what men are dead,
   Or who's alive; we must not know
   The latest books, the latest show:
We have "The Evening Post" instead.

In which the Huns delight to tell
   (Their execrable English airing)
   How badly all our friends are faring,
While all their friends are doing well.

From now, henceforth, our Island is
   Doomed to abysmal ignorance,
   Becoming, as the years advance,
A "Home for Ignoramuses."

The method of getting this result was the confiscation of all wireless receivers, coupled with the imposition of terrific penalties for any who might fail to hand in their sets on the appointed day in June, 1942.

So seriously did they take the thing that, when some indiscrete fellow, over-daring, put out a circular casting doubts on the legality of their action, they promptly imprisoned ten well-known men*, all of whom were not even suspected of complicity. They then issued a notice to the effect that, unless the " perpetrator " was handed over, the ten hostages would be sent to an internment camp on the Continent, and if there was any more trouble of a similar kind, the number would go up to twenty. Fortunately, the discovery of the real culprit put an end, after a few days, to this demonstration of the practical working of a " solemn guarantee of the liberty of all peaceful inhabitants."

In their announcement that our radios, like our cameras, were to be sent in " for storage," our gaolers informed us that the apparatus remained our property, returnable to us, and that their action was *not* to be construed " as a punishment." What it *was* intended to be has never been made clear. We know that the inhabitants of France and other countries have not been similarly penalised. In passing, it should be mentioned that the " storage " of our wireless—for which we got no receipts—has been followed by the " adoption " of many of the best sets by the Germans here, for their own use, and the export of hundreds of others to—presumably—Germany. So much for their " solemn guarantee " of our property, whatever their strict powers under International Law may be !

In any case, if the *real* idea were to stop people from " listening in," it has not achieved its end. If it were rather to give the Gestapo an excuse for terror-

---

* The owner of the name appearing at the foot of the dedication on page 2 was thus, amongst others, given his first opportunity of gauging the amenities of the Public Prison that is so much admired by all visitors to Gloucester Street, St. Helier.

izing and bullying the civilian population, it has done its work well. From the Gestapo's point of view, every civilian on the Island is now an active criminal and can be treated as such, since there is not one of us guiltless of " passing on " news, which is nearly as culpable as its reception. We are all of us liable, at the least, to imprisonment, so the Gestapo, free to pick and choose, are in clover.

It is no longer safe to know anything, or to talk to anyone in the street. The sprinkling of Quislings and Judases that is to be found in every population is coining money and laying up an ultimate prospect of tar and feathers. Anonymous betrayals are encouraged and open treachery is highly rewarded. If the Gestapo see two or three people in interested conversation, their favourite method is to wait till the group disperses and then tackle its members singly. If these disagree as to the subject discussed, it may be fairly safely assumed that it was really " news." Then very severe pressure is brought to bear to trace it to its source. There have been many arrests ; many awards of long periods of strict imprisonment, but despite it all there are still quite a lot of wirelesses in regular use.

We do not know exactly what is to be the true fate of those caught " listening in " or spreading news. We only know that, in the first place, they are sent to prison in France, but our limited experience is already enough to make us wonder whether this is the end, or only the beginning, of their punishment. When the allotted sentence has been served, will these people be sent home,† or will some new charge be trumped up as an excuse for holding them still longer in slavery ?

† Later events proved that many were, in fact, condemned to death, being moved on from place to place till they finally succumbed at one or other of the Concentration Camps.

STREET CORNER CONVERSATION

The other day I chanced to meet
A friend, while strolling down the street,
We stopped ; and to each other said—
" Good morning, George ! " " Good morning, Fred ! "
" The news is pretty good ! You've heard
About the Russ— ? " " H'sh ! Not a word !
Wait till those Jerries have gone past "

" I think the rain has stopped at last ! "
"Ah, well ! the dust has needed laying,"
" The weather—" " Well, as I was saying,
The Russians have surrounded— " " Mind !
That fellow coming up behind ! "
" Which ? " " That one, in the yellow boots !
He's one of those Gestapo brutes ! "
" I really think he's watching us ! "

" P'raps so ! And then I missed the bus
And had to walk three miles " " Well, now
He's out of hearing. Tell me how
The Russians managed to—Oh ! blast !
" Wait till he's gone ! Well, now at last
I think we're safe ! " " No ! There's that Lorna !
She's loitering just round the corner.
You know they say that it was she
Who gave away— " " She's coming ! " " We
Are growing fifty plants this year."
" I hope she didn't overhear ! "
" Who are those fellows ? How they stare ! "
" Look here ! We must go in somewhere.
I know a little place, quite handy
Where we can get a drop of brandy ! "
" Of course it isn't brandy really ! "
" It's applejack, or very nearly."
" It's only four and three a nip ! "
" These prices give a bloke the pip ! "
" We can't stay here ; we'd better shunt ! "
" Oh ! Come along then ! "

                   [*Exeunt.*]

—"IN ANY CASE, IF THE REAL IDEA WERE TO STOP PEOPLE FROM 'LISTENING IN,' IT HAS NOT ACHIEVED ITS END."

Unposted Letter No. 5. *Jan., 1943.*

THE VALUE OF A NAZI GUARANTEE

The rape of the Wireless did not provide us with the year's only example of what a "solemn guarantee" means to the Nazis. In fact, in 1942 the news, from the German point of view, began to deteriorate; Hitler must, in 1942, have realised that, sooner or later, he would be beaten; and so, in 1942, the varnish wore off, the veneer broke away, and the ugly underlying cross-grain began to show itself.

We ought, perhaps, to have been more deeply moved than we were by the horrible plight of the Russian Prisoners—some fifteen hundred men, women and children—who were dumped far from home on Jersey and, half-clothed and less than half fed, set to forced labour, or—to be candid—slavery.*

But this did not affect most of us *personally*. In fact, we have heard or seen little of the Russians except occasionally when, desperate with starvation, a few have escaped from their "pen" and subsisted by petty thefts from fields, larders and chicken runs. It needed a glimpse of the possibility of finding *ourselves* in somewhat similar case, to make us realise what that would mean.

And we had not long to wait.

On September 15th, with as little warning as is given by a flash of lightning coming out of a clear sky, wholesale sentence of exile (and in some cases, as it turned out, of death) was promulgated through our daily paper, in the words :—

"By order of higher authorities, the following British Subjects will be evacuated and transferred to Germany :

"(a) Persons who have their permanent residence not on the Channel

---

* It was only much later on that we learnt that this is a gross understatement. The Russians were beaten, tortured, brutally murdered by the dozen, and not even decently buried.

—THE RUSSIANS WERE BEATEN, TORTURED, BRUTALLY MURDERED BY THE DOZEN.

Islands, for instance, those who have been caught here by the outbreak of war.

"(b) All those men not born on the Channel Islands and 16 to 70 years of age, who belong to the English people, together with their families.

"KNACKFUSS,

Oberst."

From that moment a reign of terror began. The wolf-pack of the Gestapo was let loose upon the trail.

Very soon it became known that the orders from "higher authorities" were not as stated. They had presumably been put into the quoted form so as to cause the maximum distress to the greatest possible number. The real instruction was *not* to transport *all* in the two categories specified, but to transport a definite number of them. What that number was, or where they were to go, we were never clearly told, so the sword of Damocles hung for weeks over every head. The Gestapo made the most of the position, using it as a means of persecuting anyone who happened to be on their bad books. Victims were chosen without rhyme or reason—some were taken and others left, but none knew why.

Within an hour the pogrom had started and, once started, it went on without intermission. Even at midnight and in the small hours of the morning unfortunates were knocked up and given only a few hours in which to make ready. It was, of course, impossible at such short notice to put things in proper order, to make provision for the care and keep of dependents and of animals, or of houses and other property during the owner's indefinite term of absence. The problem of financial provision for the "deportees" themselves was simplified by the order that no one should take more than ten marks (21s. 4d.) with him. As for luggage, it had to include whatever was wanted for a three-days journey and was subject to the practical limit of what the traveller could carry, which, at any rate in the cases of elderly people and young children, meant a very small allowance indeed.

The deportation involved the immediate breaking up not only of homes, but often of families, some members of which happened to have been born outside the Island or to have fathers or husbands born elsewhere.

The first batch of some hundreds of innocent convicts was herded into a shed on the quay on the afternoon of September 18th, and thence, after an interminable wait, crowded in dirty weather on to a couple of unclean tugs almost destitute of even the most elementary decencies of accommodation. A few invalids and old people broke down from sheer physical inability to carry on and were sent back for medical attention. The rest grinned and bore it with such stoicism that even some of the Germans expressed surprise at their stubborn pluck, grim flashes of humour and solid determination to avoid any display of feeling that might have rejoiced their torturers.

The tugs could not accommodate all who had been called up and the residue, having been ordered back to homes certainly stripped of food and probably of furniture, were notified next day to be ready to go through it all again on the 25th.

Meanwhile, the visitations continued and hundreds more were roped in for inclusion in the next boat loads. No one knew whose turn was coming next: all they knew was that *if* they were sent away and *if* they ever got home again, they must expect to find their houses mere shells, everything of value having been destroyed, abused, or dispatched to Germany. Thousands, having packed a few essential belongings and given away others, sat waiting patiently till a guttural voice or the sound of a bell warned them that—so to speak—the tumbril was at the door. Day by day, hour by hour, minute by minute, we experienced something of the feelings that must have filled the crowds of French aristocrats in the Revolutionary prisons when the daily lists of the doomed were read out to them. To be spared to-day meant to them not a reprieve, but merely a postponement of sentence until to-morrow. So it was with us, but in our case a false alarm did not promise even twenty-four hours respite. The blow might still fall at any moment of the day or night. Then the home that had taken years to build and beautify would be broken up in a few seconds; cherished ties of love and friendship would be sundered, perhaps for ever, in no more time than it took to listen to a few short words—" You will be ready," and so on !

For no less than three weeks we were stretched upon the rack and then, quite casually, we were told we might get down ! The " quota " was—*for the time being*—filled ! So the shed was emptied of its " surplus stock," roughly dismissed to return to fireless and foodless homes, to jobs resigned and places already filled by others.

For many weeks, still, the sense of imminent doom hung over the Island. No one could tell when another " quota " might be called for ; when more parents would be torn away from their children, more husbands separated from their wives ; more homes irrevocably broken up. But two things we now know beyond any dispute : the exact value to be attached to a Nazi's " solemn guarantee " ; the German " higher authorities' " conception of what is meant by " liberty " !

The Germans in authority on the Islands—a " quota " was drawn from Guernsey too—must have known perfectly well where the " deportees " were going, but to reveal the knowledge would not have fitted in with their national policy of inflicting mental torture on every possible occasion. Consequently— perhaps intentionally—the most horrible rumours were circulated. Just at this time our air force had begun to strike really hard at the industrial centres of the Ruhr and the Rhineland, and many people were firmly convinced that our " deportees " were being shipped to those centres with the deliberate intention of getting them killed by their own friends.

In actual fact, it seems that they were taken to ordinary internment camps in Southern Germany, possibly with the vague idea of using them in connection with some scheme for the exchange of prisoners. But this is mere conjecture. All we *know* is that they have gone and their place knows them no more.

—CROWDED IN DIRTY WEATHER ON TO A COUPLE OF UNCLEAN TUGS.

SEPTEMBER, 1942

THE DEPORTATION FROM TWO POINTS OF VIEW:—

1. That of an enthusiastic young officer of the German "Army of Occupation" in Jersey.
2. That of a Civilian who, having said "Good-bye" to friends at the Harbour, is undergoing the mental torture of indefinite waiting for a sudden summons into exile, with or without his family.

1. FROM THE GERMAN POINT OF VIEW.

If you would be a Nazi Chief, you've got to learn—

> THE
> RULES.
> ───
> ARRANGED BY
> DR. GOEBBELS
> FOR THE USE
> OF
> HITLER SCHOOLS.

For every aspirant must take an elementary course
In "What to do with promises"
and "How to rule by force."

For instance, if you happen to have promised somebody
To safeguard with the utmost care his life and property,
Your subsequent procedure, to attune with Hitler's code,
Is to go and bash his front door in and kick him down the road.

But first you sneak his cycle—and his car, if it will go—
And, after that, his camera—and then his radio—
You promise to return them all, but that is just a ramp,
Seeing you mean to pack him off to an Internment Camp.

You give him six hours' notice, or perhaps a little less,
In which to clear things up at home and close his business,
Collect his gear, and see his bank, and find some friends who say
They'll keep an eye upon his house when he has gone away.

This mild precaution makes you smile, because, when you are sure
He's really gone, you just drop in and steal his furniture.
His interest in all such stuff is really very small:
He won't be back for years—and, p'raps, he won't come back at all!

> *But, anyhow, he's lucky that he's not been shot at dawn;*
> *Proved guilty of the ghastly crime of being British-born!*

2. From the Jersey point of view.

They are gone! They have had their last glimpse of the Town.
  They are herded like steers in the tramp's fetid hold,
Where she swings to the gathering storm, battened down—
  So they part from their country; the young and the old;

The men and the women; the rich and the poor;
  The child and the elder; the whole and the maimed;
Giant-strong in their weakness, and keyed to endure,
  That the pride of their birthright shall never be shamed.

They are singing the songs of the Country they love;
  They are hiding their misery; acting their parts,
With the heathens' black Swastika flying above,
  But the cross of Saint George blazing red in their hearts.

Their fields and their paths will be sprouting with weed;
  The ash settles cold in the desolate grate;
But deep in the spirit of man swells the seed
  Of burning resentment and turbulent hate.

It shall bloom among those who have gone in the ships;
  Among those who are left till—it may be to-morrow!
Whose fierce eyes are full, though we smile with our lips,
  That the hun shall not gloat o'er the signs of our sorrow.

Where the homes of our friends stand deserted and bleak,
  We wait in our agony—tortured but mute—
The doom that may come in a day or a week,
  To slake the insatiate lust of a brute!

There are sins past forgiveness! The die has been tossed
  And we hold by its verdict! The swine, that are steeped
In their Fuhrer's foul wallow, shall learn to their cost
  That the hatred they sowed shall most surely be reaped!

THERE ARE SINS PAST FORGIVENESS!

Unposted Letter No. 6. *Jan., 1944.*

INTERMEZZO

At the very outset of the Occupation of Jersey, the Germans made it abundantly clear that they intended to bestow the inestimable boon of permanent citizenship of the Third Reich on the fortunate inhabitants of the Channel Islands and to free them, for good and all, from the hated yoke of England. With this benevolent object in view, they naturally felt that it behoved them to educate us up to the lofty position that Providence (through Hitler) had so generously destined for us.

They started, as I think I mentioned in a previous letter, by offering the Islanders the privilege of social intercourse with the officers and men of " the Army of Occupation," organising dances and other gatherings as " meeting grounds." The success of this move did not come up to expectations, since ninety-nine per cent. of the population—some of them after nibbling at the bait and arriving at the conclusion that the proposed " intercourse " was not to stop at dancing—declined to play. Only a comparatively few girls of the lowest type reacted to the dual appeal of a uniform and ready money. Some of these, in due course, have been responsible for bringing into existence a certain number of infants that, judging by their parentage, may be expected to grow up into fairly creditable Nazis, but their number has proved far from adequate to leaven the whole mass of Jersiais to the desired degree.

The seductive strains of German Military Bands discoursing sweet music in the Royal Square, and the studied politeness of all ranks when about the town were no more productive, and those in authority soon realised that something further must be done if the people of Jersey as a whole were to be taught truly to appreciate the advantages of being insolubly linked with the world-conquerors who deigned to show such prompt and unstinted admiration for the beauties—natural and artificial ; animate and inanimate—of the Islands.

The next move must have been fairly obvious to any conscientious student of the Nazi Bible. Clearly it consisted of the judicious (and otherwise) application of Propaganda. Here the language difficulty stood in the way, but was not insurmountable. It could be, and was, tackled from one angle by making German a compulsory subject in all the schools. However, you can take a horse to the water, but you can't make him drink, and the unwilling assimilation of the German tongue by intentionally obtuse children seemed likely to be a slow process. Fortunately, another and a quicker line of approach was available.

By taking over the control of our daily paper, "The Evening Post," the requisite large and repeated doses of lies, so ably recommended by the author of "Mein Kampf," could be forcibly administered. No one could risk avoiding a sight of the Germanised Journal, since it was made the only official medium for the issue of proclamations and warnings of which ignorance was dangerous. Thus, to be sure of disseminating the Nazi culture thoroughly, it was only necessary to appoint a German Editor who could write English, or something rather like it. This gentleman, knowing that the only way to impress a German is by an exhibition of brute force, naturally assumed that the reactions of other nations must be identical with his own. Evidently, then, he must clench the mailed fist and roar aloud of blood and annihilation till his audience, thrilled to the bone, cried, "Let him roar again!" Consequently, in the columns of our "Evening Post," the armies and navies of Britain—and, later, of her allies—have been exhaustively and repeatedly "annihilated" with what were euphemistically described as "heavy bloody losses." In the intervals between recurrent sinkings of the British fleet, the armies of Russia in particular have been verbally reduced to mince-meat—and sanguinary mince-meat at that—about once a week.

As a fair sample, I take the following verbatim from the "Post" round about August, 1941 :—

"Soviet resistance may continue for a short time, but their position is hopeless. . . . The Russian forces have been systematically annihilated. . . . Besides the heaviest, bloodiest losses of the enemy, more than 40,000 prisoners have been taken. . . . The bloody losses of the Soviets are huge."

Once in a way our Editor, roaring after his prey, has roared up the wrong street. For instance, there was the occasion on which, following an effective allied air-raid over Germany, he breathed the awesome warning that "retribution will fall upon the Anglo-Americans, as surely as the sun rotates about the earth."

Yes, quite! But no more so!

More and more frequently, of late, the "heavy bloody losses" have been on the wrong side and the German official communiques have had to admit that "acting under orders, our gallant defenders have taken up new pre-determined positions further west. Our movements were not impeded by the enemy."

Probably not! They may even have been accelerated by him!

A MARKET QUOTATION.

A farmer of St. Martin,
  Who found that trade was slack,
Decided he would start in
  The market known as " Black."
Now all his pigs, it's stated,
  And all his cows and hosses,
Have been annihilated,
  With heavy bloody losses.

This change of the tide synchronised fairly closely with the wholesale " borrowing " of our wireless. It may be that those who were willing that bad news should reach us were not equally ready to grant facilities for the distribution of good news !

One has also noticed lately that the Germans are becoming very worried for fear Great Britain may not be given a fair deal by her allies when the war is over. We are constantly being fed with articles that emphasise the unscrupulous behaviour of the United States and of Russia towards the poor, helpless little British Empire !

Meanwhile, every care is taken that we should neither hear nor read anything that might prejudice our education in the beauties of Naziism. Everything intended for publication in Jersey must first be submitted to the German Censor. This gentleman, I imagine, is guided by a rigid set of rules which tell him just what may or may not be permitted ; what subjects are to be encouraged and what are taboo. The results are curious. Things that one would have thought completely harmless are turned down ; things that might have been expected to arouse the wrath of any loyal follower of Lance-Corporal Shuggelbruger are passed without question.

Let me illustrate my point.

In response to an invitation to write, for the local Pantomime, a comic song with a chorus in which the audience might join, I churned out the following innocuous jingle :—*

> *For leeks I am constantly looking ;*
> *They have such a succulent savour ;*
> *And when the potatoes are cooking*
> *They give the mild mess quite a flavour.*

---

* On Nov. 13, a " ration " of 6 ozs. of onions was issued to all adults at the price of 4½d. Subsequently, even the keenest scent failed to locate onions anywhere in the Islands and leeks soon became equally rare.

> *I wander all day round the markets,*
> *And wait till each stall-holder speaks*
> *And tells me once more*
> *What he told me before,*
> *That I lack luck when looking for leeks.*
> *Though I hunt them for days, and pursue them for weeks*
> *I dislike lacking luck when I'm looking for leeks!*
> *"Oh, yes, Sir! We have no bananas!"*
> *The shopman politely declares,*
> *"No Camembert cheese! No duck and green peas!*
> *No rabbits! No apples! No pears!"*
> *I've not had an egg for a twelve-months!*
> *I've not met a chicken for weeks!*
> *I've not even seen*
> *Such a thing as a bean*
> *And I lack luck when looking for leeks.*
> *Now that onions are short as a Hielander's "breeks,"*
> *I dislike lacking luck when I'm looking for leeks!*

My mistake lay in tactlessly telling the people of Jersey that there was a local shortage of certain foodstuffs. Of course, if I hadn't blurted it out, it would never have got known, and it was most undesirable that any impression should get about to the effect that any territory in German occupation was other than amply stocked with everything! So my poor little effort at a harmless joke was summarily turned down.

A month or so earlier I submitted to the Censor the libretto of a light opera, "The Paladins." The whole plot was in the nature of a parable, telling of the efforts of a prisoner to gain his freedom and help to defend his country. The finale told of his success. One of the songs pointed so straight towards Great Britain that one imagined it had no chance of being " passed for publication." It went like this :—

Mine is my country to love ;
Mine are the hills and the dales ;
Mine the cool uplands above ;
Mine the fresh flowers in the vales ;
Mine to protect in her need ;
Mine to defend and to save ;
Faithful in word and in deed ;
Free as the wind and the wave.

(Chorus)

Faithful and Free !
Faithful and Free !
Sure as the pulse of the tides of the sea,
That, beating around her,
For ages have found her
Strong to stand,
Motherland,
Faithful and Free !

Still, though he settles or roams
Lands that are distant and wild,
By the red roofs of her homes
Motherland calls to her child.
By the bright dews of her dawns ;
By the wet winds in her trees ;
By the lush grass of her lawns,
Draws she her sons to her knees.

(Chorus)
(As before.)

(The following verse was added late in 1944, and was *not* submitted to College House) :—

> *We, who have groaned in our chains,*
> *Sighing in vain for release,*
> *Held, through the mist of our pains,*
> *Faith that our sorrows should cease.*
> *Raptures that Freedom can give,*
> *Born of our travail shall be,*
> *Soon, when the Faithful shall live*
> *Free, in the land of the Free!*
>   (Chorus)   (As before.)

One might have thought that the references to " red " roofs, " bright " dews, " wet " winds, " lush " grass and surrounding seas would have led our Censor to the conclusion that the song referred to Great Britain and must therefore be " black-balled." But no ! The words were put into the mouth of a legendary Paladin of Charlemagne, and Charlemagne is claimed as an Emperor of Germany —crowned, as he was, at Aix-la-Chapelle. So the whole thing was approved for production without a murmur and was subsequently publicly performed† before consistently crowded houses, the song " Faithful and Free " being invariably encored on account of its patriotic sentiment and admirable music.

In passing, I must remark that the Jersey standard of theatrical production and performance is astonishingly high. I doubt whether any other place of comparable population can approach it. This has been a great blessing throughout our imprisonment, for the frequent good production of a variety of shows, ranging from Shakespeare and Grand Opera down to Charley's Aunt and Pantomime, has materially relieved the awful tedium of our existence. And, by the way, another pastime in which the Island excels is billiards. I have

† The Romantic Light Opera, " The Paladins," the beautiful music of which was composed during the occupation by Mr. P. G. Larbalestier, was first produced at the Opera House, Jersey, in October, 1943.

never anywhere seen such a high standard among amateurs and there are many worse ways of spending an evening than in watching a heat in the Jersey Billiards or Snooker Championship.

But to get back to my point, which is that the effect of a long and regular course of German propaganda on the people here has been negligible, or even negative. It has, in fact, made many more enemies than friends, and has gathered under the sign of the swastika nothing much more than a small mixed bag of misers, traitors, harlots and Judases. Some few in these categories have marketed themselves, their honour and their reputations—all articles of very trifling intrinsic value. It would be wrong to say they have " given away " their friends and neighbours : they have preferred to sell them. There is always a modicum of such refuse in every community and it is to their greed or spite that many good Jersiais owe the fact that they are now undergoing absurdly severe sentences of imprisonment for trivial, or purely technical, offences against German orders.

I am inclined to add so-called " conscientious objectors " to my short list of undesirables. This I do, not so much on general principles as because the majority of those imported here from England near the beginning of the war cannot, in my opinion, claim to be " conscientious " at all. Excused military service in return for their undertaking to help food production by devoting themselves to agricultural work, most of them took the first opportunity of imitating the Germans' idea of how a " solemn guarantee " ought to be treated. It would not be fair to make this condemnation of " Konschies " absolutely general. There are, I have no doubt, a few genuinely conscientious objectors in Jersey. There are some who have never given any undertaking as to what they would do in the way of war service. A few *may* have sufficiently strong religious scruples to justify their behaviour.†

† One at least, as we learnt later, risked his neck by secreting a Russian prisoner who had escaped from the Germans.

But these exceptions do not upset the general rule that, taken as a whole, the " Konschies " in Jersey are a thoroughly undesirable crowd. Some have toadied to the Germans ; some have gratified their " high-brow " literary tastes by stealing quantities of valuable books from the Public Library ; some have preferred to make quick money by dealing with the enemy in the Black Market, rather than to help produce the crops without which their compatriots could not keep alive. No ! By and large, I don't like them !

Within a year, very few were still working on the land ; far more had wormed themselves into soft and lucrative jobs and some had temporarily advanced their interests by " making up " to the invaders. I can only hope that people will enquire carefully into the records of such gentry before offering them, when the war is over, jobs that might surely be more advantageously filled by men who deserve better of their country.

"WITHIN A YEAR, VERY FEW WERE STILL WORKING ON THE LAND."

KONSCHIES.

Of un-Conscientious Objectors
We have a good stock, second-hand;
For someone imported
Two hundred assorted,
And someone allowed them to land.
They had promised to work for the farmers—but such
Little details don't worry their consciences much.

Go, seek them in second-hand book shops,
Reclining in masterly ease,
Surrounded by tomes
Sneaked from other men's homes
When the latter became "deportees,"
But please don't expect them their muscles to harden
By manual work in the field or the garden.

Go seek in the House of the College†
(For Fritz, after all, is a brother!).
You may find a pair
Who await on the stair,
Herr Oberst Von Something-or-other.
For they gen'rally get on quite well with the Huns;
Which is odd—since they much prefer butter to guns.

Go, seek them in Cabaret "green-rooms,"
Go, seek them in hot-rhythm bands;
Go, seek them (in shorts),
Masquerading as "sports"
Among sun-bathing girls on the sands.
Go, seek them where Nancy-boys giggle and smirk;
But for God's sake don't seek them where men really work!

† The School House of Victoria College was taken over for the staff of the Feldcommandantur.

UNPOSTED LETTER No. 7.   *Sept., 1944.*

   The long-looked-for Invasion of Europe by the Allies has come and, from Jersey's local point of view, gone. On the morning of June 6, after a night during which the undulating roar of planes, the unsilenced rowdyism of motor cycles, the barking and rumbling of guns and the grinding and grunting of heavy lorries put paid to any idea of sound sleep, we went out, to find the Germans buzzing like multitudinous swarms of bees.

   I imagine that the Commandant, like the hero of one of Stephen Leacock's stories, mounted his horse and galloped away in all directions. If not, it was only for lack of a sufficiently ubiquitous horse. His men, though busy as bees, seemed to have little of the bees' instinct for knowing each his job and getting down to it. They dashed about with ammunition, guns, tanks and everything else they had at their disposal, in all directions and back again. They evacuated hotels and bivouacked in the country as a preliminary to re-occupying the hotels. They dug trenches with spades, pick-axes and great energy wherever there seemed to be room for trenches and then hurriedly half-filled them up and dug others somewhere else. They stuck bunches of leaves in their helmets and sprayed laden branches over their vehicles, in the vain hope of making themselves look like ivy bushes and their armoured cars like sylvan grottoes.

   Meanwhile, planes droned high overhead, guns fired spasmodically and the essence of the news, with a certain amount of unwarranted embroidery, spread like wildfire through an island fondly imagined by the Gestapo to be destitute of wireless. Whatever the B.B.C. had to say was common knowledge through-out Jersey inside ten minutes and, in the general excitement, everyone forgot that he was supposed to be blindly and blandly ignorant of it all.

We thank the men who had the pluck
  To keep their wirelesses intact,
  And—risking capture " in the act "—
Have listened in and chanced their luck.

To them we've owed, from first to last
  The fact that, somehow, all the stock
  Of news released at nine o'clock
Has reached us by a quarter past!

Somehow *it spreads throughout the town*
  Somehow *the country gets to know—*
  Which very clearly goes to show
You cannot keep a good man down!

Our " Official Organ " was hours, or rather days, behind the times in its futile efforts to grind out its German tune effectively enough to make us believe the invasion a failure from the first. The hot news through the air preceded and discounted the cold print that followed haltingly. Touring maps of Normandy made a sudden appearance on the walls of sitting-rooms and offices, with place-names impudently underlined, revealing forbidden knowledge. No one doubted the success of the invasion; the question, to us in Jersey, was simply, " Which way will they go ? Straight towards Paris, leaving the coast opposite Jersey outside their orbit ? or South-Westerly, sweeping the Cotentin and " (as we confidently believed) " automatically freeing the Channel Islands ? "

Jersey must be untenable by anyone who could not hold the Cotentin coast or, at least, the neighbourhood of St. Malo. If the latter fell, any garrison left on Jersey would be isolated and would no longer be of any military value.

Day by day, the war gradually drew nearer to us. The ground quivered and reverberated to distant explosions. Then came the sound of big guns far away

—TO FIND THE GERMANS BUZZING LIKE MULTITUDINOUS SWARMS OF BEES.

across the water and at intervals the louder clamour of coast defence, of anti-aircraft and of ships' armaments far nearer. The nights were often disturbed not only by the frequent and sometimes disputed passage of planes, but by the noise of small Naval actions. German ships were attacked and sunk within sight of our cliffs. Civilian refugees and German wounded began to come in from Cherbourg and small German armed craft took refuge in our harbour. Cherbourg fell to the Americans and then, after a little interval, the advance down the Cotentin began.

Now was surely the time when the German garrison must leave Jersey if their high command set any value at all upon their services on some other front. Further delay and they would be hopelessly trapped ! And most of us felt sure that, if the enemy lost this last opportunity, an Allied landing headed by air-borne troops would soon follow.

Carteret fell to the Americans. Then Coutances. Then Granville. Now S. Malo was the only line of escape from Jersey open to any force not possessing full command of the open seas. We believed our deliverance to be a matter of days. We prized open the last long-cherished sixpenny tin of tunny fish, pulled the half-cork out of the penultimate bottle of thin red " ration " wine and feasted recklessly, in anticipation of freedom and plenty.

Expectations and wishes in Jersey varied. Some expressed the hope that our Germans would be trapped and beaten in the Island itself. Others, some of whom had memories of street-fighting elsewhere, would have preferred our garrison to attempt an escape and would have welcomed a night of big explosions, signifying the preliminary destruction of their dumps and harbour equipment.

While our fate hung thus in the balance, we remained very, very near the front line. The sound of gunfire was almost continuous. Allied planes crossed and circled the Island, apparently as and when they pleased, whether flying high or low. We were daily eye-witnesses of demonstrations of Anglo-Saxon aerial

—THE NIGHTS WERE OFTEN DISTURBED NOT ONLY BY THE FREQUENT AND SOMETIMES DISPUTED PASSAGE OF PLANES, BUT BY THE NOISE OF SMALL NAVAL ACTIONS.

supremacy, culminating one sunny morning in a sight never to be forgotten by us prisoners, in whom a mere glimpse of any sign or symbol of our own people could never fail to arouse feelings of joy and pride.

This time, instead of the drone of planes rising and, a few minutes later, dying away in the distance, the whole atmosphere seemed filling up with sound, developing into a deep continuous, drumming diapason. A steadily growing crowd was gathering where a street debouches on the harbour and the sea. "There they come!" cried someone, "I've counted four hundred and fifty already!" I followed his pointing finger and his example and, late-comer though I was, was in time to figure up a further six hundred and ninety. All the air seaward was speckled with Allied planes and, as I looked, more and yet more kept darting into sight over the bluff of Fort Regent, where German guns were silhouetted against the sky, manned but impotent. Still they came.

> *Flight after flight and squadron after squadron;*
> *Orderly wedges, perfect in formation;*
> *Mounting into hundreds, soaring into thousands;*
> *Glinting in the sun haze, gleaming in the sunshine;*
> *Stretching their wings like gulls above the water;*
> *Sweeping from the Eastward, stately and unchallenged,*
>   *Emblems of air-power.*

A few more days passed and now the noise of war came to us from the south rather than the east, and the news was of rapid advances throughout Brittany and Normandy. From the high ground behind St. Helier one could see great columns of smoke and flame rising vertically, perhaps nearly a mile high, over St. Malo and Dinard, followed minutes later by the rumbling roar of distant explosions. The Americans were there; and never before had we so fully realised the essential unity of the Anglo-Saxon race.

FLIGHT AFTER FLIGHT AND SQUADRON AFTER SQUADRON.

But all this time, how many of our people's young lives are being sacrificed ? Ought we to glory in their great deeds, or rather to mourn over the losses they must have sustained ? The men who have died did not ask for glory, any more than for pity. And somehow it seems to me that, while glory is their just due, pity—and the sort of grief that is bred of pity—would be abhorrent to them.

Blow, Bugles, blow !
Sound the " Last Post,"
Above a silent host ;
Down the still gardens where, till wars shall cease,
Our galaxy of heroes rests in peace ;
Waiting the day when, echoing through the blue,
The great " Reveille " burgeons forth anew.
Blow, Bugles, blow !

Blow, Bugles, blow !
Is Death so dread ?
Salute the glorious Dead !
Trumpets triumphant, thunder forth again ;
To greet the apotheosis of the slain,
Who pledged their youth to Freedom, or the grave ;
They saved the world, themselves they could not save.
Blow, Bugles !
Wake, proud trumpets !
Sound once more !

Still our " Army of Occupation " showed no signs of leaving. In fact, by now it had been reinforced by a heterogeneous influx of whole and wounded soldiers from the Cherbourg Peninsula and by Naval men, numbering perhaps a couple of thousand, the crews of armed trawlers and small war-ships of various kinds, incapable of finding any way home after reaching our harbour.

Soon the later stages of the battle of France were in progress and the excitement of the news, coupled with the probability that our people might still decide to take the Island by assault, obscured in our minds, for a time, the fact that the war was moving rapidly away from us and we were still prisoners and likely to remain so for months to come, unless a sudden breakdown of the German war machine were to bring the whole thing to a quick end.

Now the noise of the guns has died away in the distance. Our planes no longer incite the German A.A. batteries to paroxysms of futile barking. Silence has succeeded sound, as autumn has ousted summer. The sickness of hope deferred has followed the exhilarating excitement of expectation. We are, for the time, in worse case than ever before. The great tidal wave of war has passed us by, leaving us in a stagnant backwater, our shores, as it were, littered with the flotsam and jetsam of the German débacle.

Their high command has been so incomprehensively stupid as to leave, perhaps, sixteen thousand fighting men marooned on an Island so placed that they can no longer take any part unless our people choose to force it upon them. The troops here are, to all intents and purposes, prisoners ; and we are the prisoners of prisoners. Our friends can only reach us by blowing up our prison with us in it. Our thin lines of communication are cut ; our trifling sources of supply have dried up. No letter, no message, can reach or leave the Island. Surely, no ordinary prisoner of war is so rigidly isolated from all the outside world !

Low in the West
A blood-red sun lies dying,
Mourned by the murmur of the evening breeze.
Our homing thoughts,
Like pigeons swiftly flying,
Stretch their winged shadows o'er the parting seas.
What shall we find,
When Freedom's bright to-morrow
Lifts the dark veil from off the welcome shore?
Must fires of joy
Be quenched in seas of sorrow,
That friends who once were ours are ours no more?

Some there may be
With countless duties cumbered,
Or gripped in coils of closer hopes and fears
For nearer ones
And dearer; so have numbered
Long severed friendships with the forgotten years.
Others there are
Who, in the spirit, voicing
The ageless honour of their breed and birth,
For friends that live
Laid down their lives rejoicing—
Man hath no greater love than this on earth.

LOW IN THE WEST
A BLOOD RED SUN LIES DYING.

Unposted Letter No. 8.   Jan., 1945.

COLD, FAMINE AND SQUALOR

The last few months of 1944 have been, for us in Jersey, a period of gathering gloom, only relieved by a gleam of light at the very end of the year. To begin with, the weather broke up early and it rained more or less—generally more—every day for nearly three months.

Ever since early September, the great majority of us have been habitually hungry, increasingly cold, generally wet and never clean. We have not suffered from lack of food alone, but equally of fuel, of clothing and of soap; in fact, of almost everything. And nearly every week something else is missing from the very short list of the comforts that remain. The gas mains were finally emptied as long ago as September. The water mains only function for two or three hours a day. The supply of current from the Electric power stations has just ceased and the telephone service is to stop in a few days' time. The Island's stock of coal and coke is exhausted and there is no longer any household ration of wood fuel. The steam laundries are closed down and hand laundries cannot work, for want of soap and fuel. Personal cleanliness is out of the question.

In the absence of firing, it has been impossible, during the wet weather, to dry damp clothes. The average man's wardrobe is as bare as his cupboard, so the expedient of wearing a different—and possibly well-aired—suit is generally out of the question. What clothes are left are worn out and cannot be replaced or even mended. The odds are at least ten to one against the possession of a pair of boots or shoes that will keep out the wet.

Those whose houses are not fitted with electric light—and they are many—have nearly all been condemned to darkness from sunset to sunrise for months past and now all of us are in the same boat. Oil is nearly unobtainable; a few candles have changed hands at as much as £1 apiece; to get a small box of safety matches one must pay at least a shilling and flints for lighters are even more difficult to obtain than petrol.

It is a wonder that there has not been more illness, particularly among children. Their feet and bodies have been constantly cold, wet and dirty; their clothes both filthy and inadequate; their diet deficient in many ways. Add to these facts the almost complete absence of medicines, antiseptics and the like and it remains a crowning mercy that, up to now, the Island has not been swept by an epidemic.

Efforts have been made to combat the combined shortage of food and of fuel by opening a number of communal restaurants and by instituting about fifty bake-houses to which the housewife may carry a utensil holding the food to be cooked, subsequently calling and getting it home as nearly warm as distance and delays permit. Either method of getting food does not, of course, increase the individual's ration. Both entail frequent walks in all weathers, a great hardship to the old, the infirm, and anyone " on the sick list."

What with perpetual fetching and carrying of unsatisfying meals, the worries and delays of " queueing up," the struggle to make ends meet, and the impossibility of safeguarding the children's health and providing them with anything approaching enough clothing, the life of the Jersey housewife has little to commend it at the moment. Try as she may, she and her family, day and night, indoors and out, cannot—as I have said—be other than hungry, cold, wet and dirty.

Meanwhile her husband, in threadbare clothes and leaking boots, is ill-equipped for any outdoor job. He must, however, not only get his work done, but do it on meals the material for which, for the entire day, aggregates, on the average, about

> A quarter of an ounce of meat,
> An ounce of breakfast meal,

> Ten ounces of bread,
> A quarter of an ounce of butter,
> Half a pint of milk,
> Half a pound of potatoes,

and any other vegetables, mostly roots, that happen to be obtainable. His first meal is taken before sunrise—probably in the dark ; and his last not before sunset—probably in the dark again and most likely in wet clothes. All are distinguished by a complete absence of sugar and of salt and are washed down with no beer and followed by no smoke. After his evening meal, he can choose between going out into the dark roads and remaining at home in the bosom of a wet and irritable family collected in a dull, damp house and slowly drying its dirty clothes and boots in the only possible way ; namely, by the somewhat odiferous process of exhalation of such heat as remains in their half-starved bodies.

About the beginning of September the Bailiff, on behalf of the Superior Council of the States of Jersey, submitted to the German Authorities a memorandum which very ably summed up the situation and the International Statute by observance of which it should be remedied. "It is," he wrote, " an undisputed maxim of Public International Law that a Military Power which, in time of war, occupies any part of the inhabited territory of an Adversary is bound to provide for the maintenance of the lives of the civilian population of the occupied territory." This, he pointed out, the Germans were no longer able to do ; therefore their occupation of Jersey should cease. His statement made it quite clear that the lives of the population were already endangered and the danger was increasing day by day. Medical supplies of all kinds, including anæsthetics, were nearly exhausted ; so also were soap and all cleaning materials. The institution of Communal Ovens would " place an increasing strain on people already under-nourished, under-clothed and ill-shod." The hardship resulting from lack of heating would increase till mid-winter. Many supplies would soon be completely exhausted ; sugar by mid-November, salt soon after that, butter before the end of the year, coal and coke by December, wood fuel by November and one or two more small rations would see the last of coffee substitute, macaroni, dried beans, cheese, tinned fish, matches, oil and saccharine. As to clothes, the Island held material for 2,500 shirts against an immediate demand for 18,000 ; 250 pairs of trousers against 5,000 pairs, leather for the uppers of 3,000 pairs of wood-soled shoes of which 13,570 pairs were immediately wanted for children alone. There were no materials available for making suits, dresses, or overcoats.

After recording the fact that, during the occupation, the people of Jersey had " grievously suffered in both body and mind," the Bailiff concluded with a solemn warning to the German Authorities in the Island. The day, he wrote, would come when the Powers would meet " to pass judgment upon the Authorities, be they civil or military, upon whose conception of the principles of Honour, Justice and Humanity the fate of Peoples and of Places, and, not least, of Occupied Peoples and Places, has temporarily been determined. May the Insular Government be spared the duty of adding to the problems which will face the Powers an allegation that . . . the Military Representatives of the German Government unnecessarily endangered the health, and indeed the lives, of the People of Jersey."

A few days after receiving this memorandum, the German Commandant issued a notice to the effect that it had gone forward to his government, by whom it was being submitted to the neutral ".Protecting Power." This seemed to imply clearly that our acute position would at once be made generally known and, one imagined, something would be done for us without delay. For a time we waited hopefully. Then, for a time, we merely waited. When November came, and still no word of help, we began to despair. Could it be that our own people for some reason would not, or could not, come to our aid ? Day by day our position was growing worse. The depth of the winter lay before us. We were faced with starvation by a combination of cold and hunger and apparently no one cared what happened to us. The morale of the people sank to a lower mark than ever before.

NOVEMBER, 1944.

No sunlight gilds the bleak November day,
Cows give no milk and bees produce no honey;
(And I have often noticed, by the way,
November nights are also far from sunny.)
Fowls lay no eggs—there are no fowls to lay,
So, if they did, it would be rather funny.

I own no garments to compare with those
A self-respecting chimney sweep might wear,
No boots, no braces and no Sunday clo'es
Revealing merely normal wear and tear;
While, as for trousers, goodness only knows
When, where and how to find a decent pair!

I have no meat, no sweets, no drink, no smoke!
My grate reveals no single glowing ember!
There is no gas, no wood, no coal, no coke!
No warmth, as in the days we all remember!
No water and no soap! No lights! No joke!
No—vember!

There is a well-worn saying to the effect that it is always darkest just before the dawn and this has certainly proved true in our case. About the middle of November it became known that the Bailiff's memorandum had never reached its promised destination. The States met the Germans afresh and this time something really *was* done—the memorandum was broadcast to the world in clear Morse. It was no longer possible for any ill-disposed individual to sever the chain of communication. Soon we learnt that the International Red Cross was bestirring itself on our behalf and on the last day of the year there arrived in St. Helier's harbour from Lisbon, a Swedish vessel, the "Vega," bringing—as a first instalment—parcels of food in the care of Red Cross Representatives empowered to examine our conditions and take further steps for our relief. It is no exaggeration to say that our feelings are comparable to those of a condemned prisoner reprieved on the morning of his execution.

THE RED CROSS.

I.

A day there was that knew no dawn. That day,
For three tremendous hours the sun was cloaked:
Deep darkness brooded over all the Earth,
That groaned and trembled; and the Temple's veil
Was rent asunder.

                Then, above the mirk
That hung impenetrable, grey as smoke,
Round the black cauldron of the dull Dead Sea,
Slow rose the sun, a ball of lambent fire
That glowed tempestuous in its molten shroud
And lit the rugged timbers of a cross
That stood upon the Hill of Calvary
Stretching its supplicating arms abroad
And throwing back the rays incarnadined.

Then they whose eyes were fastened to the ground
Saw nothing but the darkness of the tomb;
But they whose heads were raised in hope, beheld
A Red Cross, spreading light athwart the World.

FOR NINETEEN HUNDRED YEARS AND MORE
THE BLOOD-RED CROSS HAS STOOD BEFORE THE WORLD
AN EMBLEM AND A SIGN OF FAITH; OF HOPE.

II.

Time sped. For nineteen hundred years and more
The blood-red Cross has stood before the World
An emblem and a sign of faith ; of hope.
It glowed upon the banners of the hosts
That sought, in simple faith, by force to rend
The City of the Holy Sepulchre
From Paynim hands and, by the the gift of blood
Spilled freely for the cause, to justify
The mad tribunal of unlovely war.
It blazed upon the surcoats of the Knights
Who tarnished Suliman's magnificence,
That strove to force upon the Western World
Islam's fierce faith.

    They of the Red Cross struck
The blows that saved the soul of Christendom
And swept the Crescent from the tideless sea.

So that wan captives, blind from living death,
Dazed by the radiance of unwonted day,
Out of the darkness raised weak hands to praise
The Red Cross, spreading light athwart the world.

III.

But now, when all the awful arts of war
Have reached a foul perfection of their own;
When every child and every woman shares
The dangers of the soldier under arms;
When flying death sweeps, shrieking, down the sky;
When fertile lands and ancient cities, rich
In all the treasured beauties of the past,
By sudden cataclysm overwhelmed,
Are changed to desert wastes and noisome heaps
Of mangled filth—the badge of the Red Cross
No longer decks the slayer in his pride,
But stands the symbol of a fellowship
That takes no lives, but freely gives its own
That friend, and foe, may live; whose work it is
To lay cool hands upon the fevered brow;
To soften the last agonies of death;
To ease the lot of those who must live on,
Maimed, blind, unfitted for the work of life;
To link the prisoner with long-lost friends;
To feed the famished and to warm the cold.

Therefore, let all of us who prize the gifts
By love bestowed, by kindliness inspired,
Unite in thankfulness to praise and bless
The Red Cross, spreading light athwart the world.

UNPOSTED LETTER No. 9.   May, 1945.

We are Free ! After nearly five years " in Jail," Jersey is Free ! The little islands that were William the Conqueror's before ever he fought at Hastings, the oldest inheritance of England's King, are no longer under the heel of England's arch-enemy ! We are FREE !

The Union Jack is flying over the Royal Square and, by its side, the Stars and Stripes. It is flying, too, from the Town Hall, from Victoria College, from Fort Regent, from Elizabeth Castle, from Mont Orgueil, from—but it would take less time to tell where it is *not* flying !

On Hitler's birthday, last month, when the Germans tried to hoist their heathen Swastika over the fort, the halyard jambed and the emblem of the Crooked Cross drooped prophetically at half-mast throughout the day. Now it has gone for ever, and so has the man whose vicious rule it symbolised. The dead hand did not lie long on Jersey and there was no ill-omened hitch when, at ten o'clock on the morning of Wednesday, May 9th, the Union Jack was broken at the masthead of the Royal Court !

We are Free ! Did Freedom come to us officially on May 8th, or May 9th, or May 10th ? I am not quite certain. On May 7th, Winston Spencer Churchill—the greatest of all the Churchills, which is saying a good deal—announced that the German surrender would " include Norway and the Channel Islands." Then, at three o'clock on VE day, he told us that " hostilities end officially at one minute after midnight on Tuesday, May 8th, . . . and OUR DEAR CHANNEL ISLANDS ARE ALSO TO BE FREED TO-DAY." On that day, too, the first British Troops landed at St. Helier Harbour. Later, we learnt that the German Major-General Heine did not sign the unconditional surrender of the Islands (on an up-turned rum barrel on *H.M.S. Bulldog*) until 7 a.m. on Thursday, May 10th. So how do we date our Freedom ? But who cares ? WE ARE FREE !

—NO LONGER UNDER THE HEEL OF ENGLAND'S ARCH-ENEMY!
WE ARE FREE!

Hail, the day of Freedom's dawning,
Freedom we have craved so long.
All the harbingers of morning
  Wake the world with joyous song:
Calling loud from every tree:
        We are free!
        We are free!

List! The woodlands join the chorus,
  As the winds that fill the skies,
Parting noisome mists before us
  Stir the leaves to lisping cries;
Sing of happiness to be;
        We are free!
        We are free!

Ransomed daughter of the ocean,
  Hark! Your mother wakes from sleep;
Wakes to blend in grand commotion
  All the voices of the deep;
Breakers roaring from the sea:
        We are free!
        We are free!

"Ducks" are waddling ashore and along the Esplanade. Huge landing craft, stranded head-on upon the beaches under West Park and First Tower are disgorging welcome cargoes from their gaping mouths. British battle-dress is to be seen everywhere. The hated "green-fly" is being rapidly fumigated out of existence. We can say *what* we like, *when* we like, *where* we like, and as loud as we like. After nearly five years of silence and of hushed whisperings, we can shout the truth on the streets and from the house tops by day, from lighted windows by night, unrestrained by black-out, by curfew, by suppression of wireless, by the constantly present horror of the loathsome Gestapo! WE ARE FREE!

And just at the moment when Freedom came, there came also our old friend, the *Vega*, unloading yet more Red Cross supplies at the very moment of our great deliverance. And once again let it be put on record that we can never repay our debt to the Red Cross that, in the hour of our greatest need, relieved the tense misery of us all and saved very many of us from a lingering death.

But do not imagine for a moment that the simultaneous coming of the New Year and of the new hope brought to us by the Red Cross meant a sudden and final ending to all our trials and troubles. Not at all! The Germans saw to it that we should not be given too much cause for rejoicing. They themselves were so short of food that they badly needed the small stocks still held in store for the civilian population. Having collaborated, in their own interests, in getting the Canadian and New Zealand "Prisoner of War" parcels to us, they were able, without actually murdering us wholesale by starvation and incurring the inevitable penalty, to take for themselves what little of *our* food there was on the Island. This they did and presently our ration of flour ceased altogether and we were left without bread for about three weeks, until the *Vega* again came to the rescue with a cargo of flour, as well as a further supply of parcels.

By that time the Germans had decided that we no longer deserved, or needed, any of our own potatoes. Green vegetables being off the market, we then became horribly dependent on a mash of swedes served thrice daily. Then even swedes ran short and, for the last fortnight of the occupation, very many families had to subsist solely on their ration of bread and a couple of pints of milk a week. There have been periods during the last few months when working hours had to be reduced because the men were not getting enough food to make a full day possible.

We grew so weary of it all that we felt—doubtless mistakenly—that we should have welcomed the expected " Battle of Jersey " for which we have now learnt that our people were trained to the minute, even knowing more of the lie of the land and the location of the German defences in the Island that we did ourselves. But we could do nothing but wait.

The worst thing about this last stage of our imprisonment has really been the mental strain, the futile speculation as to how it would all end, and whether we ourselves would be there to see the finish.

For some time past the German troops here had been half-starved and— many of them, at least—wholly disgruntled, with the accent on the grunt. They were, in fact, spoiling for trouble of some sort and bitterly jealous of the good food brought to us by the *Vega*. Meanwhile, most of the officers, so far as we could judge, remained determined to hold the Island to the last gasp, whatever force might be brought against them. They did not believe the unconditional surrender of Germany as a whole to be a possibility, and had made up their minds that, so long as any German resistance continued anywhere, they would hang on to their one little bit of British Soil.

Thus it seemed that we were faced with a somewhat unhealthy alternative ; either a mutiny in our midst, with the certain accompaniment of street fighting, looting and murder ; or else an invasion in force, inevitably involving a prolonged and bloody battle for one of the strongest strong-points on the western sea-board.

Daily the German troops grew more and more restive. They were paying through the nose for food, smoke and drink. Local grown tobacco was fetching £40 a lb. and a raw apple spirit (Calvados) a dollar a small "nip." Corn was gladly bought at a £1 a pound, when it was obtainable at all; eggs, if any, sold at over six shillings each. Dogs and cats were kept carefully indoors, but somehow managed to stray by hundreds into German cooking-pots. The men dug up seed potatoes as fast as they were planted, munched raw swedes and regarded stewed stinging nettles as a luxury.

This state of affairs led naturally to an epidemic of burglary and theft throughout the Island. Day and night, German soldiers not only sabotaged the crops and pillaged vacant houses, but found or forced their way into occupied dwellings and stole food, money, or anything marketable. In many cases their behaviour was such as could fairly be described as "robbery under arms," and old and helpless people were treated ruthlessly and sometimes brutally assaulted.

By the time March came, the atmosphere, in German quarters, was becoming highly charged. So highly that one morning the Palace Hotel exploded with a loud bang and a wide-spread rain of debris, just while a meeting of their own officers was going on in it. This, of course, was a mere coincidence, so "mere" that rumours of its forthcoming occurrence were rife two or three days in advance.

From time to time, German soldiers distributed leaflets among their comrades and along the road. One of these—in rhyme—ran thus :—

GEBET DES JERSEY SOLDATEN.

Komm, heiliger Hitler, sei unser Gast
wo sind die Dinge, die du uns versprochen hast ?

Wir sitzen hier in Jersey allein
und laden Dich zum Essen ein.
Bei Ruebensuppe und Brennesselkohl
fuehlst Du Dich bestimmt auch wohl.
Mit Sieges versprechen und Hassgeschrei
schlugst Du Europa und Deutschland entzwei
Der deutsche Soldat, der fuer Dich sich einst schlug,
hat von Deinen Luegen mehr als genug.
Und wenn dann in Deutschland ist aus der Traum,
komm hier zu uns, wir finden " nen Baum
wir haengen Dich auf mit Deinen Knechten dazu
und dann ist Schluss und die Welt hat Ruh " !

This, being interpreted, means—to the best of my belief—

Thrice-holy Hitler, be our guest !
Come, bring with you your forecasts fine,
And join us, with the greatest zest,
In Jersey, where we sit and dine
On noxious stews of roots and petals,
On chunks of swede and stinging nettles.

No longer can you feed us up
With victor's boasts and shrieks of hate.
Your soldiers know they've bought a " pup,"
So now we're not disposed to wait
While you, devoid of truth and wits,
Break us, and Germany, to bits.

We've had enough of all your lies;
So come, and we will find a tree
From which our leaders, brave and wise,
May dangle very prettily
You and your gang! Then wars shall cease,
And we—and all the world—have Peace.

Later on it was reported that May day was to witness the rising of the majority of the German troops against their officers; then that the date would be further postponed until the fall of Berlin. But all along we were rather sceptical about the whole thing. The Germans are such worshippers of discipline, so thoroughly trained from childhood in unquestioning obedience to the word of command, that we could not help feeling that, when it came to the point, they would rally behind, not against, their officers; just as their kindred had been doing for long months past at St. Nazaire, L'Orient and Dunkirk.

In that case the end of our imprisonment must be an invasion, a fight for the beaches, a costly advance, accompanied by bombardment from land, sea and air; a house to house struggle for St. Helier, the wrecking of the Harbour, the fortifications, the town; our houses probably reduced to rubble, our furniture to kindling wood; ourselves—many of us—dead among the debris alongside of our rescuers and our gaolers. Only by a miracle, it seemed, could some such climax be averted.

And now the miracle has come! There is no need to tell of it; for the whole world knows and rejoices. Germany has at last broken under the intolerable strain: broken and crumbled into dust! And so we are free! Jersey is free! Not only Free but—incredible as it seems—bearing no visible sign of war wounds save for a few trifling scars. And even these, in course of time, will disappear, or, maybe, will come to be prized as reminders of five years of trial and tribulation endured, on the whole, with creditable fortitude and loyalty.

Jersey, like every other country, has suffered from the curse of a quota of traitors, quislings, common — mercifully *un*common — informers, Judases, profiteers, dregs of all kinds. But she can be proud to number among her people many heroes who have earned that title not only in the heat of battle, but by brave and patriotic actions, performed day after day in cold blood and with the knowledge that detection meant solitary confinement, torture, death. Of such are the men and women who have defied and outwitted the all-powerful Gestapo ; who have protected the helpless and sheltered the escaped prisoner ; who have accepted unmerited blame and punishment that others should go free ; who have carried on stubbornly in comfortless homes on starvation diet, giving the best to the children ; who have risked and borne imprisonment and ill-usage that they might bring to others the cheer of good news ; who have hardly existed on a pittance rather than be well-paid and well-fed in return for work helpful to the enemy.

Yes ! By and large, the record of Jersey during the occupation is one of which there is no need to be ashamed, and one not unworthy of the great loyal traditions of the little island that still acclaimed a king and abominated a dictator even when, for a brief spell, England herself would have no truck with monarchy.

And now ; Jersey is Free ! No longer have we cause to cry " Haro ! Haro ! A mon aide, mon Prince ! "

We are FREE !

OPEN GATES!

Open are the gateways to the highways of the sea;
Let us forth in Freedom with the legions of the free!
Open are the pathways to the ends of all the world,
    Where the flag of Freedom is unfurled,
Brushing from our boundaries the walls that hemmed us in:
      Let a new life begin!

Shattered are the ramparts that were shaped by lust of power;
Greed has lost its mastery, and pride has had its hour.
Long down-trodden nations have arisen in their wrath,
    Scattering the tyrants from their path.
Broken are the barriers that kept us from our kin;
      Let a new life begin!

"WHO, RULING, SERVES"

We, who are freed from bondage, know full well
The cruelty of dictatorial rule;
The mental torture of a code that breeds
Mistrust between the father and the son;
Hate between neighbours; shrinking fears that wake
Hideous suspicions.

                        And full well we know
There is no better code in all the world
Of men who value Freedom more than life
Than that of monarchy, beneath a King
Who rules but, ruling, serves; whose steady mind
Dwells not in palaces,† but rather loves
The simple homes of "ordinary"† men;
Who studies steadfastly, in earnestness,
To do his Duty in that state of life
To which his God has called him; and who asks
That men should do no more, no less than this.

† At about the time of his Jubilee, King George V said: "I don't know why they make such a fuss of me. After all, I am a very ordinary sort of fellow!"
At about the time of his Coronation, King George VI remarked that he and his Queen were not "palace minded."

FAITHFUL & FREE

from "The Paladins"

Words by
HORACE WYATT.

Music by
P. G. LARBALESTIER